The Illustrated
Alphabet

of
FLOWERS

Eve Heidi Bine-Stock

A a

ASTER

A is for Aster

Try to remember
To give it to someone
Born in September.

B b

BLUEBELL

B is for Bluebell

In woodlands of the British Isles,
The ground is thick with flowers
Under the trees for miles and miles.

C c
CROCUS

C is for Crocus

In early spring this flower shows
And oft is caught
In winter snows.

D d

DAFFODIL

D is for Daffodil

Gifting these flowers in a bouquet
Marks ten years of marriage,
With joy every day!

E e

EVENING PRIMROSE

E is for Evening Primrose

It blooms in the night
With bright yellow flowers
That close when it's light.

F f

FUSCHIA

F is for Fuschia

Eat its berries, some are sweet.
In homemade jam,
They're quite a treat!

G g

GERANIUM

G is for Geranium

It's the leaf, not the flower,
That's the secret which gives
The fragrance its power.

H h

HIBISCUS

H is for Hibiscus

Known for its bright hues,
This flower is used in China
For polishing their shoes!

I i

IRIS

I is for Iris

Its name means "rainbow" in Greek
For its many colors of blooms.
And its stunning shape is unique.

J j

JASMINE

J is for Jasmine

In India, it's called "Queen of the Night,"
That's when its scent fills the air,
Calming us down so we can sleep tight.

K k

KANGAROO PAW

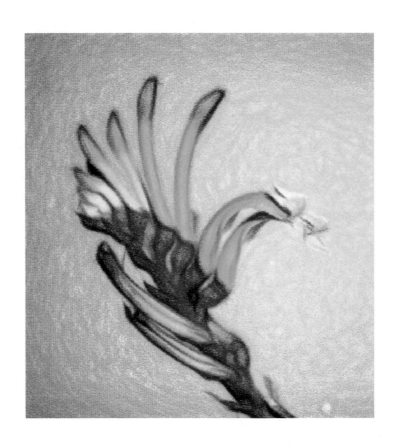

K is for Kangaroo Paw

A Western Australia native,
Its pollen is carried on a feeding bird's head,
Such teamwork is so creative!

L l

LOTUS

L is for Lotus

Grows in waters shallow,
Its flowers rise above.
For Hindus, this bloom's hallow.

M m

MIMOSA

M is for Mimosa

A fluffy flower growing where hot,
Its leaves fold up when touched,
Hence the nickname "Touch-me-not."

N n

NASTURTIUM

N is for Nasturtium

Put these cheery flowers in a salad bowl,

They will taste like pepper

And their taste you will extol.

O o

ORCHID

O is for Orchid

Some grow in the air
Without any soil,
For flowers, that's rare.

P p
PEONY

P is for Peony

It can be as big as a cabbage,
And comes in all colors but blue,
It bespeaks of a happy marriage.

Q q

QUEEN ANNE'S LACE

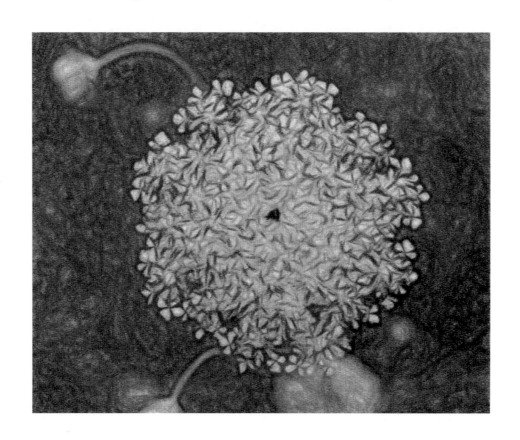

Q is for Queen Anne's Lace

This frilly flower looks like lace,
But is truly a wild carrot,
And oft is added to a vase.

R r

ROSE

R is for Rose

You must be forewarned,
Although they're so pretty,
Most roses are thorned.

S s

SUNFLOWER

S is for Sunflower

It moves with the sun
From the east to the west
Until day is done.

T t

TULIP

T is for Tulip

Its bulb was once sold
For more than the price
Of less precious gold!

U u

UVA URSI

U is for Uva Ursi

It's also called "Bear berry"
Because bears like the fruit,
So if you approach, be wary!

V v

VIOLET

V is for Violet

Chosen the state flower of Illinois

By a majority vote in 1907

Of every school-age girl and boy.

W w

WISTERIA

W is for Wisteria

A kind of pea, it grows on vines,
Can live a hundred years,
And 'round and 'round a tree it twines.

X x

XEROPHYLLUM

X is for Xerophyllum

Early explorers misnamed it "Beargrass."
It's not grass, and bears don't eat it!
Glacier National Park has it en masse.

Y y

YARROW

Y is for Yarrow

Also called "Carpenter's weed,"
It treats a cut
So it won't bleed.

Z z

ZINNIA

Z is for Zinnia

This type of flower is called, "Cut and come again."
The more you cut, the more it blooms,
Cut five blooms, and soon will grow ten!

68581389R00018

Made in the USA
Columbia, SC
08 August 2019